I0489148

7 EASY TIPS TO **SUCCESSFUL**

ENTREPRENEURIAL
JOUNEY

A REPORT ON STARTING YOUR OWN BUSINESS

S. BARATH

First Printing, 2015

Printed in INDIA

TABLE OF CONTENTS

7 Easy Tips to successful Entrepreneurial Journey

Introduction

Today, as we are living in the 21st century many countries around the world are struggling to become great economies and people around the globe wanting to become rich and wealthy and the way to make it is only by becoming entrepreneurial and only by becoming entrepreneurial, it is very much possible to become rich and wealthy.

In 7 Easy Tips to successful Entrepreneurial Journey we would be going into the story, philosophy, psychology, principles and strategies of entrepreneurial thinking and how one can transform to become a great entrepreneur!

Story

Let me just introduce myself.

I am a middle class Indian born in India and went to an engineering college and a second tire Business school and having worked on various jobs I finally landed myself as a solo entrepreneur!

In India and in particular southern part of the country they have always believed in jobs and job security and often parents would always want their kids to become Doctors, lawyers and engineers because it allows job security and so, people like me who want to become entrepreneurs have to break the old paradigm and to believe in entrepreneurial thinking!

I myself have addressed thousands of college students this last year alone in the state of Tamil Nadu in promoting entrepreneurial thinking among students and faculties!

I was also a principal Advisor to the southern nodal centre of EDI Ahmadabad and was involved in transformational initiatives in improving entrepreneurial thinking among young minds and also as a faculty to EDI Tamil Nadu I have also have done many programs on entrepreneurship for students and young entrepreneurs alike!

I started my first business when I was just 29 year old along with two other senior partners and after a year we parted away because we almost had no business...we created a so called a product and it almost took around 6 months to do the prototyping and another 6 months to know that it would not sell!

After my first experience as an entrepreneur went back to corporate for another 3 years before I tried my next business and this time I never partnered with anyone but built a training company and have been successfully in business for the past 5 years! In these 5 years I got the opportunities to work with more than 20 corporate clients, 60 plus colleges and universities and have trained lakhs of students by now!

Why am I writing this book? I am writing this book because I would like to give the fundamentals of starting and running a business with very less capital in hand.

When you have very little money and want to start a business it is always challenging and I have seen so many youngsters who tried starting a business after quitting their jobs and miserably fail and eventually going back to corporate jobs!

So, I am going to give you all the required tools, methods, strategies for starting and running a successful start up!

TIP 1 - PHILOSOPHY

As a business man you should be having a business philosophy mean whether business is easy or difficult? What is important to you and so on?

Business is easy if you can do three things correctly, that is creating, selling and collecting

What is creating, selling and collecting?

1. Creating a product or services
2. Selling your product or services
3. Collecting cash or check and maintaining your finances

If this is so simple then why is everyone not able to do it?

Because it is not that easy,

Creating a product is first stage and you need to create a viable product where there is market potential

Manufacture the product or replicate it (production factory) to sell it!

Selling the product is the third stage

Collecting cash and cash flow management is fourth

And as an entrepreneur you may not be good at all the four things and genuinely you should answer to yourself what you are good at!

Let me put it this way,

What you need is,

- Innovation
- Product development
- Production / Manufacturing
- Sales and Marketing
- Distribution
- Cash flow management / financial management

But as a solo entrepreneur you need not be an expert in everything but you need to understand the basics of everything and should be a specialist in one thing and that one thing should be either Product Development or Marketing but every entrepreneur should be good at Marketing!

As peter ducker said Innovation and Marketing is the key to Entrepreneurship!

FINDING YOUR NICHE
First thing you need to do is to find your sweet spot that is where your passion and opportunity meets!

Most people who believe that doing what they love will solve their problems would also start doing what they love but money may not be coming...let me put like this, I like slow swimming, casual painting and slow jogging but, will it put money into my pocket just because it is my passion area? No not at all! So, it is not just following your passion but converting your passion into a profitable idea!

We should be asking "are we making money from our passion? And how much?" we should be quantifying all our income streams and find the area where we do better and focus on those areas!

But 95% of people would say why follow your passion and why not do business where there is money alone...yes, people can do it but often these are the people who shut shops within a year or two because they can't keep doing what they don't like and delivery quality results and eventually lower revenue and profits!

So, select the business where there is passion and profit together and which is not an easy task but would take some time to figure it out!

More than selecting products and services you need to select your ideal customer and to do that you need to understand your customer very well and otherwise it is often very difficult to sell.

While starting a business, setting up office space or buying furniture comes later and first thing you need to do is understand your customer.

When you think like your customer then you can easily connect with them and selling to customers who are similar like you is also a better option as you understand them better.

List down what your customer likes, reads, what associations and groups they belong to and so on...

Also what demography and other preference...

Narrow down to your ideal customer and target them!

YOUR NETWORK IS YOUR NET WORTH!

Another important thing that you need to do as a business man is that you need to develop you contacts. Whether you know it or not you contacts will determine your net worth for sure.

Once you have certain people who starts giving you business will continue to give more...and so your network matters a lot to you.

Take a sheet of paper and write all the people that you know and also people who you want to contact them in future.

Keep a list of key contacts with you and keep building that list further and further...

I also see that successful entrepreneurs find the right fishing holes and start exploiting them, what I mean is you need to find the right audience for your product and how you do is find the audience who is buying similar products like yours and understand their psyche. When you go to amazon.com you could find that people who bought that also bought this and it is nothing but the same strategy!

What if you can't create your own product? It is nothing like creating your own product, but if you can't then make a joint venture arrangement with the people who have good product suitable for your audience.

More than the product your list of prospects becomes very important and the way you build it by giving them value!

TIP 2 - BUILD YOUR WEB PRESENCE

Internet is changing the world in the way we communicate and also buy stuff and so, having a quality web presence is mandatory. What I hear from successful entrepreneurs is that having a word press site serves the purpose.

Having a capture mechanism like an opt-in is very important in capturing the leads, because Lead generation is the life blood of any business and generating leads online is a very wise decision in this information era.

Opt-in should be present both in the top of the page as well as at the bottom to make sure that maximum conversion happens

You capture leads for building relationships over a period of time by communicating through email sending useful information like articles, videos and podcast etc...

At first you should not be focusing on immediate sales but build relationship which will eventually lead to conversion later!

PREMIUM PRICING

One thing I note when I go to the entrepreneurial seminar as a speaker is that people who are just starting often think of pricing the product very low so that they have a competitive edge but actually you don't! , I will explain why...

When you price it very low you might have problem covering all your cost but if you can create a "value chain" (that is) "services at different price points" then it would be an ideal strategy leading you to better profits.

YOUR CORPORATE IMAGE

Your corporate image or your company image is very much important and you need to spend little bit money on the website, broachers, visiting cards etc...

Don't make it look homemade but make it look very professional there is a web site called printvenue.com which allows you to get customized marketing materials like visiting cards, broachers, personalized gifts etc.

When you create videos use professional camera and sound recorders. Even for podcast using a professional recording device will give you a professional edge.

Using a recording studio for recording is also a better option and there are some studios which charge very nominal and do research for those studios in your city!

WHY MANY PRODUCTS FAIL?

The reason many products fail is because of lack of product-market fit and it happens because mostly the entrepreneur thinks that his product will succeed and produces the product without any market testing and when they launch they might get surprises!

And so the modern way of launching products is by testing it in the market before it is fully created or engineered.

There is something called MVP i.e. minimum viable product which is produced and tested in the marketplace and if the results are not satisfactory we get the market's reaction or feedback to do iterations!

All those iterations can only be done, only when you know who your target market is and what they like and dislike etc…

The old paradigm that marketing is separate that of the product is gone, and we should know that the product itself is part of marketing and creating a purple cow is the new era's competitive strategy!

There is something called Blue ocean strategy and I would recommend young wannabe entrepreneurs to read Blue ocean strategy!

To know about Blue Ocean strategies do visit blueoceanstrategy.com!

BUILD A WEBSITE THAT WORKS

When it comes to building websites most businesses build a static site with no newsletter subscription or opt-in and also there is no good content to attract audience. So more than building a web site it is important to have good content through articles, videos or podcasts and also a lead capture mechanism like opt-in so that you can keep communicating with the prospect!

The marketing side of web should be given focus rather than the technical side and the sad fact is most of web development companies know only the technical side of web development!

So, you need to get updated with good web marketing strategies including creating quality content, copy writing, blogging, videos etc

TIP 3 - FREEMIUM

This is a strategy by which you convert a visitor into a potential prospect and a user by providing quality product or services free of cost!

Selling is not a one shot deal but rather it is a process and in that process the first step is to provide value to your prospect by providing freemiums like content, software, videos, audios etc and in turn get their permission to have their email ids or phone numbers etc and this is the fundamental of permission marketing. Seth godin wrote a book on this some time back called the permission marketing and I would recommend people to read it!

Converting this user into a paid customer is the next strategy and it can be achieved only when you keep communication with your prospect for some time by providing real quality value.

In the direct marketing industry they had been using something called the 3 step letter sequence and it is like mailing one letter after another which has continuity and success rate is normally high. This same strategy is now used differently by blogging/newsletter etc...

EMAIL HAS THE POWER

Even when email is old, use of email in business is very effective and communicating with your prospect using email is very much recommended!

One tip that I would recommend marketing using email is provide a P.S below the email and give your link to your download or landing page and it is a very good way to do free marketing and publicity to your audience!

ALL STRATEGIES ARE OK BUT YOU NEED EXECUTION

Just knowing all strategies is not enough because execution matters at last and making an idea into a product or executing your strategies all need the mindset of a doer and many creators start projects well but they are poor finishers and so if you need to be successful you need to become a good finisher.

So how do you get things done? There are three things that you need to have:

Firstly you need to be good at planning and spend at least 30% to 40% of your time in planning and strategizing. Putting all your process into a process flow diagram and also creating a decision tree like planning tools will help you increase your productivity!

Secondly you need to develop proper routines and habits which will double your productivity. Say example when you are creating newsletters and articles you cannot be writing them whenever you like and in that case you might end up working and not writing for some periods of time and so, have a schedule like publishing one article per week or one video per 2 weeks and so on…

Also having a schedule calendar to make sure that all important tasks are done on each day!

Thirdly your mindset is very important and ability to focus one task at a time and concentration is very critical for your success!

Being a finisher needs practice and keep practicing till you keep finishing task after task…

EXAMPLE OF A PROCESS DIAGRAM
This is a diagram that I have drawn based on my own understanding and you can draw yours as well

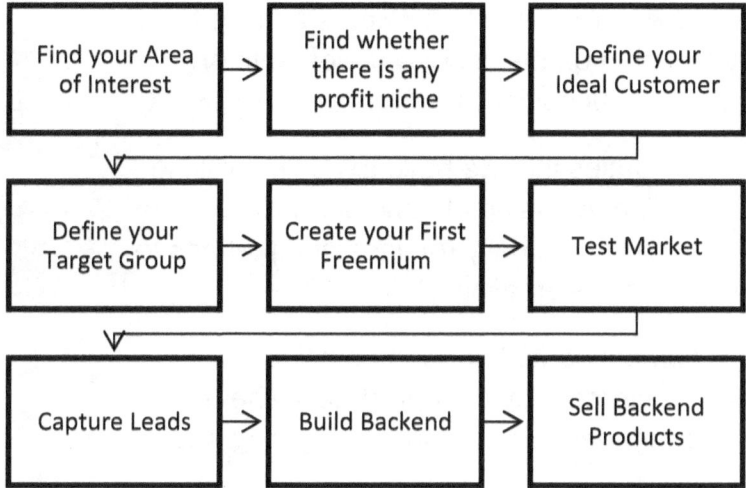

What this process diagram shows is a complete overview of small business marketing strategy and online marketing strategy!

Developing the steps makes our life easy and allows us to systemize it!

HABITS FORM THE FOUNDATION OF SUCCESS
Habits are the foundation to success in life and in business and we have to develop a very healthy habit whether it is planning, strategizing, sales or marketing, book keeping etc..

All of us are not good at everything and also it is not possible for us to acquire all the knowledge in the world but we have to know a lot about our business, our industry, our competitor and our customer.

Focus is what we miss as entrepreneurs and we have to get it by focusing on the important elements of running a successful business.

There are daily duties that we have to do like waking up, bathing, eating, dressing etc and similarly business also has some daily routines and that has to go religiously and systematically!

Business is something that happens outside of us. Only when a customer buys our product we have a business and that needs planning, strategizing and executing etc...

And so many functions of the business need to be delegated or outsourced. All things should not be done by one person rather it should be shared by many. This is a very hard transition for a solo entrepreneur and often fears of spending too much and employing others but if it is done strategically you have a better chance of growing big!

TIP 4 - LESSONS THAT YOU SHOULD LEARN FROM BRANDING

There are some fundamental lessons that we need to learn from branding, here are they:

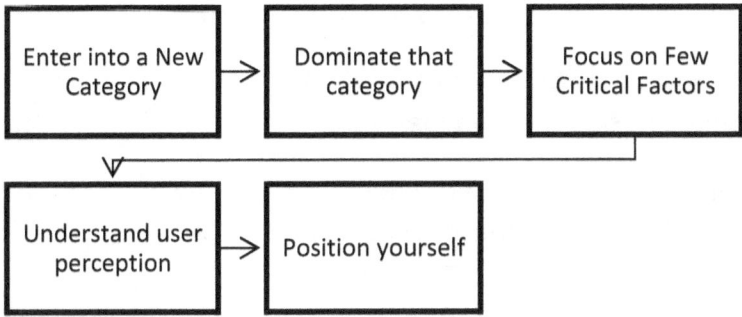

When you plan to position your brand you could use all kinds of marketing tools and ideas

Some of them are as follows:

But for all kinds of branding and positioning you need to do strategizing, planning, Getting things done and execution!

And execution is the major challenge for many small entrepreneurs

What is the easy way to increase productivity? Number one is prioritizing and planning

Appointments and meetings are inevitable and have to be recorded on the calendar. Other activities like writing, programming, blogging etc should be prioritized based on importance.

Focusing on one thing at a time is far better than juggling too many things but as an entrepreneur you might be juggling with multiple projects and so focus on one at a time.

LIST BUILDING
After doing all the website, opt-in etc you need to focus on list building and how do you do that?

The myth that the money is in the list is not completely true because the money is in the relationship that you develop with prospect and not just their contact numbers.

So, when you provide real value in terms of information, learning etc to your potential prospect will allow him to sign up your list and keep getting messages from you on a regular basis.

When you write good articles on your blog it serves as a tool for diverting traffic into your site and allows people to opt-in to your subscription

Doing videos with your website link is another very good strategy to drive traffic and today major traffic is there in youtube and so use of videos will be very effective.

When you do live speaking engagements you can introduce your audience to your web site

Be ready to write reviews, testimonials to others so that you also get a free publicity and there by generate traffic to your website

Bringing traffic to the website is itself a big subject which cannot be discussed in more details and I encourage you to study it and in particular about SEO and social media marketing etc.

How to increase traffic?

The traffic can be increased either using google adwords and other advertisements or you can increase traffic using free traffic strategies like SEO, Article, blog, Audio podcast and video which is nothing but content marketing. Through content marketing you can increase the web traffic and it is a permanent solution for all your traffic!

Knowledge vs Action

When I was watching a Jackie Chan movie he was telling a boy who wants to learn kung fu that how can you learn when your cup is full and when you know so many stuff and to pour your cup before you learn more...

And so when you keep on learning it is not enough and you need to pour your cup before it is filled again and so keep applying what you have learnt and this habit will allow you to be better at your business

There is a program by the famous internet millionaire and guru Rich schefren called GPS and in that program he says that increasing mere knowledge will not make you a doer and a successful business man and so It is not what you know that matters but it is how you think and the way you think will get you places!

In any business there might be very few important elements that would make you become very successful and those are called the critical success factors and as a business man it is your job to identify those critical success factors and focus on them.

For example when I was appearing as a visiting faculties for a business school I asked the students what made them to join the course or the b school, for that they replies that it was the Air-conditioned Infrastructure, the location, the front office counselor and next comes the faculties and teaching methods.

And so, things like infrastructure and location played a major role and these are called the critical success factors and for an online business there would be some critical success factors like your web site, newsletter, blog etc…

The time spent should be on the important things and tasks and one which will make us go to the next stage of the business. If our constraint in our business is product development then we need to focus on the product development. Even if you are outsourcing your work you need to plan everything in advance to commence the work.

In the world of Internet marketing the major work goes into content creation whether it is text, audio or video and the web site creating, design, updating the web site etc.

And in the world of marketing there are two ways of approaching marketing one is spending unwanted dollars on advertising or go for PR and content marketing which will yield long term and better results. You have to choose between quick fix vs permanent solution.

ENTREPRENEURIAL MINDSET

Being an entrepreneur is a choice and the commitment to remain as an entrepreneur is the most critical aspect of becoming successful individual.

Entrepreneur is someone who is comfortable being a solo person or an independent person and no matter what initial failures, challenges and problems he faces he should keeps going through the journey and that's the quality you need to posses as an entrepreneur.

You might be in the middle of a project or you might be heading towards a better plan but immediate results or success may not be there and people around you may be discouraging you but you need to believe in your purpose, vision and your abilities and keep going…

If you are committed and put in persistent effort then success should elude you in the course of time…

Some few years back when I was hearing Robert kiyosaki's audio I heard him speak about two kinds of people existing in the world of business, that is you are either a giver or a taker…what he really meant was a giver is someone who gives value first and then demands for his fee or payment etc but a taker on the other hand takes the money before he actually delivers value…and Robert was asking people to be givers!

So, be a giver!

A typical entrepreneur is more a impulsive, intuitive person and so he may miss all the details along the way…but if you are gifted to be more detailed person you don't need to worry about detailing but, if you are more a impulsive type then I would recommend then to focus on planning their work before they execute!

In fact I love the statement made by the CEO of bharat matrimony Mr. murugavel janakiraman during a speech at IIT Madras, he said "first jump and then figure it out…"

I think a typical entrepreneur has that mindset to jump first and figure it out along the way…but planning along the way is the discipline that we need to inculcate so that we achieve even more…

As I am writing this book, my business is also going a radical transformation…from little business now I am facing capacity insufficiency as more programs have poured in…and I need to add more people into my projects as consultants!

There are two kinds of problems in any business. One lack of orders or sales and the next is lack of capacity to deliver the excess sales that you have got….

Both problems are good and you need to work on those areas that are critical for success!

But the major problem that most people face is the former…that is lack of orders or sales!

How do you overcome that?

You will be able to overcome this particular problem only when you work on your marketing and related processes!

As an entrepreneur it is good to have the go getter attitude like jump in and do it but if we have to transform the business from a single man operation into a bigger business then planning, organizing and strategizing etc becomes very critical.

TIP 5 - Turn keying your business!

When we want to transform our business from a single man operation into a bigger business then the first step is to make the organization into different functional areas and allocate different capable people to manage it!

Say for example:

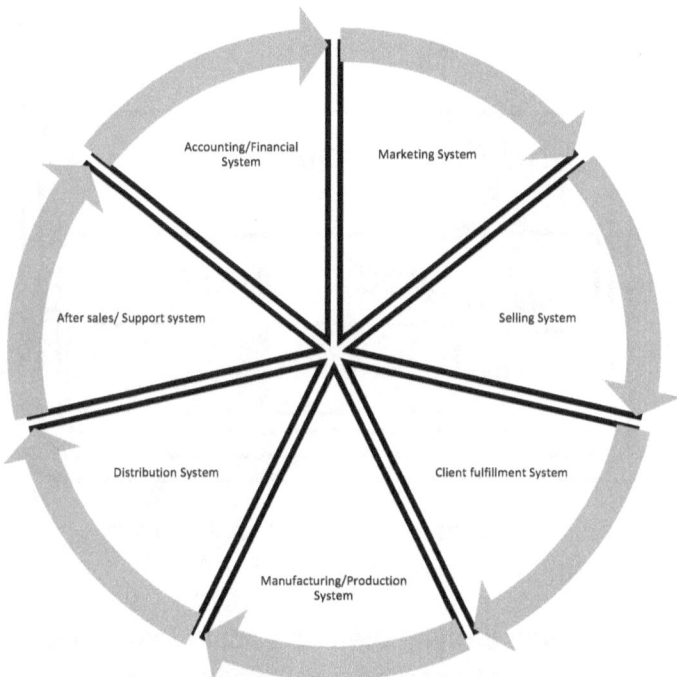

After segregating into different functions, we have to make sure that capable man power resource is allocated but then if we don't have enough capital to hire people then, we have to allocate these functions to the limited capable people in our organization and by doing that we are distributing responsibility for various roles and tasks!

Next thing that we need to do is we have to take one particular role or function and list down various tasks that are involved in it, like below:

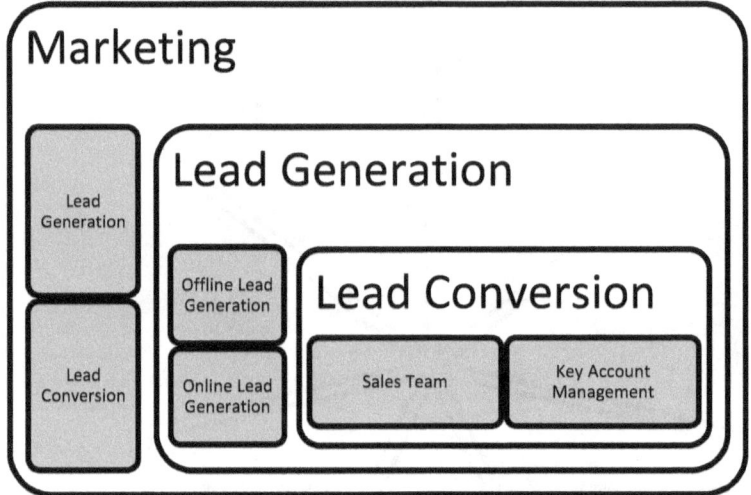

List all the activities that are involved in each step of the process! And document them!

When you develop a complete checklist of tasks that needs to be done, it becomes very easy to manage and you also will get an overall picture of your entire business.

From the checklist we should be listing them in the order of importance and there by narrowing down to few areas that matters and those are called the critical success factors for our business!

When you focus on the few activities that matters we will be able to produce phenomenal results and so it is essential to find those areas in the first place and focus on them

Also write down all the process so that we have better clarity for execution

Clarity is very much important for an entrepreneur and by writing down the various processes that are involved in a business the entrepreneur will be able to have a bird's eye view about his business

Process mapping helps to define the work involved and also helps us to delegate those tasks or outsource those tasks that are not our strength areas

Let's look at an example mapping I have done for my business:

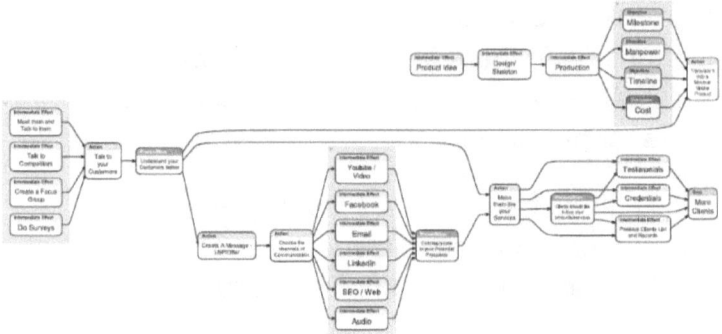

And by doing such a map it is easy to find areas that needs to be outsourced or delegated

All the planning, organizing and orchestrating talents will come only when you have the right motivation and only when you are doing what you like doing…and so, fundamentals remain the same.

VALLEY OF DEATH
Just look at the below diagram:

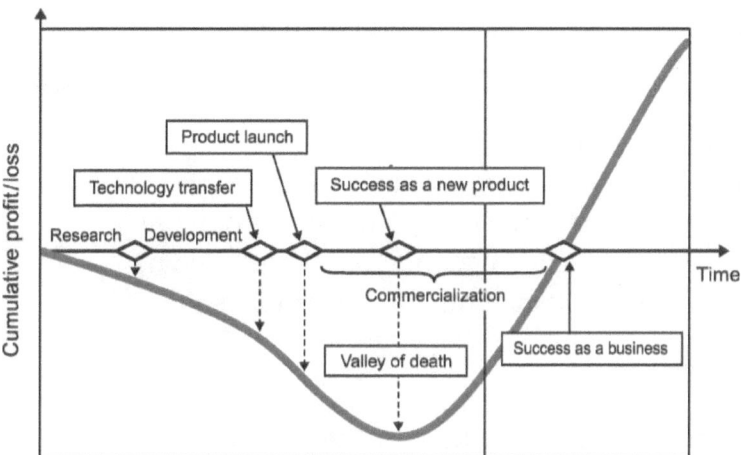

This is called the valley of death; every company has to undergo this learning curve in order to become successful

And also an entrepreneur should be willing to fail initially and undergo a steep learning curve in order to become successful

Like a caterpillar turning into a butterfly, the outcome seems very glamorous but there will be difficulties, setbacks and challenges that an entrepreneur must be willing to undergo in order to become a great successful entrepreneur!

So, the foremost prerequisite is to never give up on your entrepreneurial goals and dreams and be flexible and adaptable and make necessary changes and learning's to make the transformation from a reluctant entrepreneur into a successful one.

TIP 6 - GET A MENTOR

One of the best ways to progress is to get a good mentor. It is very true that getting a mentor is not that easy but if you are ready to spend your time in finding one it will be the best thing you can do for yourself

How to find one?

Keep searching for people who can help you in your industry and start networking with them, never try to make everyone your mentor or guru because it will not work out and so, wait for the right mentor to appear and it may take quite some time but get a good one.

Mentor should be a successful businessman and he should also be willing to allow you for an internship

Not all entrepreneurs allow others for an internship and so find the one, who would allow you to learn,

Never ask for a salary or compensation while you are undergoing your Internship or entrepreneurial training and mentoring…

The learning that you undergo with an entrepreneur and the contacts that you would get may turn out to be priceless latter on and so, just stick around for some time learning the fundamentals!

CONTROL EXPENSES

The difference between a successful entrepreneur and an unsuccessful one is everything to do with how you handle your expenses

Major expenses will be:

- Land
- Rent
- Machinery
- Raw materials
- Salary

Also you need to control

Excess inventory (wastage)

Accounts receivables (payment to be received)

Accounts payables (payments to be made to your vendors)

These will be the valuable suggestions to overcome the above problems:

- So, as an entrepreneur you have to make sure that you get advance payments and try avoiding accounts receivables,
- But it may not be possible all the time.
- Produce only required finished goods and keep very less inventory.

- Make sure you make profit and then pay your vendors and ask for a good credit payment period and method.
- When you start don't spend money on Infrastructure and big machinery.
- Rent a small place and then expand.
- Hire less people and pay them mostly on commission basis.
- More than anything increase sales

TIPS 7 - DO'S AND DON'TS OF STARTING A BUSINESS

When you start a business don't think of putting an office and buy expensive furniture's and equipments etc because these things are not going to bring in sales or profits into your organization, yes, if you happen to have a retail outlet then your appearance really matters!

Also, don't just spend your money on pamphlets and send them and wait whether you would get any response and most often the newspaper guy will deliver your pamphlets to only certain areas where he distributes and also many times they don't put those pamphlets along with the newspapers and so, avoid this ineffective way of marketing

Also, don't waste money on some classified advertisements in newspapers and expect miracles to happen…because it will never happen!

A marketing campaign will be successful only when your message is very relevant for your audience and the advertisement has to be shown to your target audience minimum 21 times or more to get a valid response

So, don't just put an ad once and expect results because you will not get any results.

Never give away a promise that you cannot deliver and if you do something like that then, your business will die very soon…

Also, don't just try copying your competitors because you may not be able to differentiate your services and also you may not be able to deliver what you are promising and so, don't just copy others

You can copy others only when you are sure you have those delivery capabilities and also if it is complimenting your internal strengths

Making money should not come first because if it is the first objective then you may not be thinking to create something of real value to your customers and so, creating something of value comes first and satisfying your customers should be the primary objective rather than mere making money.

Marketing is not pitching…

Many sales and marketing professionals do too much pitching to make the sale and this may not be an effective way to do business

Easiest way to kill a sale is by doing pitching!

At last remember that 80% of all the results comes from only less than 20% of the activities and so, find those top 20% activities that would yield results and that is the key to quick success!

20% of clients bring in 80% of sales

20% of products are responsible for 80% of the revenue

20% of the activities produce 80% of results

Find your 20%

Always ask what is your natural strengths are? And leverage on it rather than try copying others…

What comes natural to you? Those are your talents and gain related knowledge and skill to develop it into strength

Different kinds of Entrepreneurs and what kind are you?

Creator

Brand Builder

Deal Makers

Trader

Investor

Etc…

Everyone have their unique style and so, you got to find you style, the one which is working for you and so, find your unique style and leverage on it!

ABOUT THE AUTHOR

S Barath (Barath Surendran) heads a training organization called Techemate Leadership Academy (www.techemate.com) and has been into business, building start ups and so on from year 2006 onwards. He has been awarded "Star Achiever" by National integrity cultural academy, India and has been awarded the Alumni Achievement Award by ITM Business School, India. He has done corporate training programs for companies like Hyundai MOBIS, FORD, Visteon, Skill Tree, Beissel needles, SSEPL, Karya technologies, Leaap International and many others. He is also a Visiting Faculty and Consultant to Versatile Business School, Chennai.

He helps budding entrepreneurs and leaders. He is actively involved in Internet Marketing and Direct Marketing businesses. And he has created many e-businesses in the past.

You can write to him to his email id – barath.surendran@gmail.com and you can find him in face book - https://www.facebook.com/barath.surendran

Check his Website - www.minimbamillionaire.com

www.minimbamillionaire.com